Living with an
Alcoholic
Husband

A true account of living with
and without a husband
addicted to alcohol

Cherry Parker

Living with an Alcoholic Husband

ISBN -13: 978-1483956114
ISBN- 10: 1483956113
Copyright © Cherry Parker 2012

www.cherryparker.co.nz

"This above all,
to thine own self be true"

Hamlet, 1:3 Shakespeare

Please note:

The author is not a counselor, doctor, therapist, psychiatrist, life coach or health professional.

This book is my own personal opinion gleaned from living with an alcoholic partner, my husband.

For the purposes of this book the alcoholic will be referred to as "he".

If you fear for your own safety seek a safe refuge.

In an emergency the front of the phone book lists numbers for urgent help.

Seek professional people who are trained to assist you if necessary.

"To me the sound of a metal bottle cap unscrewing against a glass bottle is the worst sound in the world.

To my husband it is heaven."

Between those two sentences lies my true story, of being married to a man, whose heavy drinking eventually led to chronic alcoholism.

There are no right or wrong answers to the dilemma of living with an alcoholic. The only correct solution is the one that works for you alone.

The last few years of my marriage were difficult. Decisions to change had to be made and acted upon. And things would never be the same.
I am no expert. This won't be a fun read. You may not agree with what I have done or what I say.
That's ok. We all have the right to make our own choices, to have our own opinions.

It takes courage to admit there is something very wrong with your life. And courage to do something about it. The first step may have been to pick up this book.

It can also be frightening to read a book that reflects the bad things that are happening to you. You don't want to turn the pages but you feel you must.

If something in this book stops you in your tracks, acts as a mirror to your life, and you say to yourself "Yes that's me" read on and see what choices you have.

Change won't be immediate, but next week, next month, sometime in the future, courage will grow and you will be able to make changes that will make your life better.

You may need to hide the book. If you do, you need to read it more than you know.

Take from the following pages what is beneficial for you, what will help you the most, and leave the rest.

Sometimes it may not be pleasant to read, but nor is the situation you are living in now.

Was he Always like That?

The most common question I am asked is "Was he always like that?"

No he wasn't. I would never have married him in the first place if he had been.

I met and worked with him when I was 16, married him at 18, and had to leave for my own sanity after 34 years. In the following three years I continued to be there if needed, to offer support and at his request to manage his finances.

What some people don't ever consider is that the person does not become an alcoholic overnight. They don't go quickly from someone who maybe drinks a little bit more than others in the room, to a heavy drinker who drinks every day, to shutting out the world and drinking solidly for five days and nights.

This happens over years and years, and happens so slowly that you become used to it and it isn't noticed. All I can compare it to is going grey or gaining weight.

Suddenly one day you open your eyes and ask – "When did that happen?"

How it is Now?

The two drinks in the evening become three or four. The weekend drinking starts at 1pm instead of 5pm.

In a few months the first drink is at 10 am and before you know it Saturday and Sunday are a write off.

Then comes the drinking between work and home. Soon after the lying about the amount consumed starts and bottles are hidden in strange places – the woodpile, the lawn mower catcher and the spare wheel cavity of the car.

As the quantities that need to be consumed increase to reach the desired effect, the lying increases also.

The above process takes years and unfortunately the partner gets engulfed in the conspiracy. Then come the arguments and the confrontations. The alcoholic promises to only drink after 6pm or says that the consumption will be limited to only one bottle in the weekend.

For a very short time you are taken in by this, because you trust this person, and are unaware of the secret stashes.

Yes they do what they say – "Only one bottle in the weekend." But this should really read "Only one bottle in front of you in the weekend."

The hidden stash is always there as a top up.

The Windscreen Wiper Effect

About now the seesaw effect kicks in. Or what I prefer to call the windscreen wiper effect. Dr Jekyll and Mr Hyde.
Call it what you will.
The windscreen wiper effect flicks back and forth between the good and the bad personality.
Of course there are still good times thrown into the mix but they are becoming further and further apart.

The windscreen wiper effect starts with the alcoholic saying
- "I am going to be a different person as soon as I get such and such a problem out of the way."
-"These two bottles will last me two weeks."

The short periods of stone cold soberness between drinking binges only magnifies the good qualities that you know this person has.

So you think – "Perhaps it is me. Perhaps I am imagining it."
Maybe you have spoken to a close friend or family member, who has never seen the antics of your alcoholic partner.
They look at you astounded. "What is she talking about? He's not that bad. What an imagination."
With these thoughts churning around in your head, doubt creeps in and you convince yourself that you are exaggerating the entire situation.

Putting the Alcoholic First – Always

We continually make excuses for them.
We always put them first before making any choices, such as going out to dinner or having friends around for the evening.

The control they have when others are around, is stronger than when you are alone, because the alcoholic is sure, that rather than cause a public argument or make a scene, you will keep quiet – And you do.

The False Front

The pleasant likeable front will be maintained in public but the minute you are alone the windscreen wiper flicks aside and no matter what you say - or don't say - it will be wrong 100 % wrong.

An outing is spoiled before it begins with the knowledge of what you will end up facing.

This behavior also escalates very, very slowly. Unfortunately we get used to living this way. We slide gradually into a deep rut. We don't realize it is happening until one day the realization strikes that it really is easier not to go places – dinner, shows, any type of celebration for that matter, because to stay at home is less stressful and less embarrassing.

A Life Dominating Problem

The problem dominates your life, even though you try your hardest not to let it.

It never used to be like this. His drinking was always there in the background but it is now taking the lead role, impacting on everyday living.

I used to look forward to Friday nights and weekends. The last five years I came to dread them and looked forward to when he went back to work on Monday morning. Even a simple Saturday morning cup of coffee and a look around the shops can be utterly ruined by "I'll just buy a small bottle on the way home."

You know it will be gone by 2pm and replaced with a larger one by 5pm.

They alter our lives. Our thoughts become illogical.

They confuse, clutter, overtake and consume our thoughts. You get worn down by the good guy, bad guy, drinking, not drinking, lying, telling the truth, worry, hope, please not this time, maybe he will stop, perhaps it's me. Yes it is me. No it's not; on and on, ad finitum.

You retreat into yourself because it is more peaceful than being confrontational.

And you continue to hope. Hope that after the next promise he will really mean it. Hope that next time it will be better.

But he continues to drink. Happy in the fact that he believes he has the power and control over you that you will always keep quiet, so endorsing and condoning his right to drink.

You have always kept quiet and not told anyone before, so he continues to drink.

In fact he drinks more, tauntingly so, making a point of pouring drinks purposefully in front of you; making no attempt to hide what he is doing.

It is used as a snub, "A ha-ha I'm getting away with this. I know you don't like it, but I also know you'll do nothing about it."

Of course there are still good times along the way to really screw with your brain.

Once again you think. I must be imagining it. It's not really that bad. It is me who is paranoid.

The wind screen wiper is now at full speed and together with the moods generated by the alcoholic, you are becoming exhausted.

They Belittle and Embarrass

Their actions belittle and embarrass us.

All the time the hope is that things will improve and every time you hear "I will only have one drink tonight" your hopes are pathetically raised. He might be sober for at least tonight. The fact that this one drink is nearly all alcohol and no mixer does nothing to alleviate the fear that your partner will soon once again become this other horrible personality.

The brick that sits in the bottom of your stomach starts to remain there from first thing in the morning until he is asleep at night.

Someone to Talk to

Right – The time has come. I really must talk to someone. But because the problem has never been aired and has been cleverly hidden you are met with astonishment.

You may have chosen to talk to a close family member. Their disbelief might as well be tattooed on their forehead. It is not what they say. It is what they don't say.

What they don't say is "She's exaggerating. We know he drinks. All guys like a drink or three. What a nag. Poor guy. No wonder he drinks. She's paranoid about this alcohol thing." Perhaps it was different in my case. I had not drunk alcohol since the birth of my daughter, so some people have me in the "She's a bit weird because she doesn't drink" club.

So you go back into retreat mode.

I am imagining it – it must be me.

We continue to pussyfoot about, keeping quiet, putting up with mental abuse and despair, while the alcoholic is kicking up his heels, having a great time socially, doing what he wants and no one is standing in his way – Yet.

Both Partners become ill

We as partners and wives do not realize that we also have a problem. So much attention and time is directed at the alcoholic that we are just along for the ride. Bumpy and horrendous as it may turn out to be, we think the problem is not ours.

We need to face the fact that although we are not the alcoholic we do also have a problem. A problem not of our own making, but one that we need to address.

At the beginning, although if you asked me I couldn't pinpoint the beginning, I would have said that I didn't have a problem. It was all with the drinker.
But once again slowly, slowly the alcohol continually in the drinker's system starts to change the brain and the way that they think. The personality ever so slowly starts to change, starts to split into two people – two personalities.

We who live with them in turn live in a constant state of anxiety. This brings about physical illness such as headaches, breathing problems, poor appetite, stress and sleeping difficulties.

Because you are constantly living on a knife edge each and every day, every hour, wondering what personality they will be today, tonight or in the next hour, you also begin to live in fear and constant anxiety.

All this leads to a major state of "unwellness." Your self confidence is stripped away, and a feeling of being able to accomplish anything other than the basics is impossible.

With the bad occurrences of the past repeating themselves ad nauseum into the future, they befuddle our brain into seeing no way out.

The pretext of keeping up a front to the world is exhausting.

I call this *"My Concrete Umbrella"*

My Concrete Umbrella

It is the only way I can describe the feeling.

The weight of the problem caused by alcohol is heavy. Very heavy. It presses down on you from above. Not on your shoulders but from a few feet above your head.

For some unknown reason a pretence (or so we think) needs to be maintained and presented to the world outside our small sphere.

Presented to the great "They" out there.

The people who we think are watching and judging us.

On reflection, three years later who "They" are is unfathomable to me now, and if I could have named them, did they really care?

Their own problems were most likely keeping them well occupied.

Anyway, to maintain this pretence I had to hold these problems at bay. Couples all around laughing and chatting, sharing and smiling. They didn't seem to have one of these umbrellas. Or did they?

But who knows. No one could see mine either.

15

Two Inseparable Personalities

I cannot separate the two personalities that are standing in front of me in one body.
This person who is being mentally abusive, foul mouthed, an obnoxious drunk, this person who is not the person I married. He sometimes reverts back to a semblance of that original person but he is becoming more and more this new monster.
Someone who I wouldn't have married. Someone who I would now cross the road to avoid, or scurry down another supermarket aisle, leaving my purchases and heading for the car. Someone who I am ashamed and embarrassed to be with. This new person lies, torments, bullies, cannot be trusted and thinks only of himself.

Where is the love, the caring for me, the friendship, the love, the stability, the laughter, the love?
When did I last laugh with this person?
A person who loves you does not act like this.

It is said they are sick. All I know is that he is making me sick too. Do I have to live like this just waiting for the sober moments? Will he ever be really sober again?
How long do I have to wait?

This verse used to hang on the dining room wall.
Don't walk in front of me, I may not follow.
Don't walk behind me, I may not lead.
Just walk beside me and be my friend. - Albert Camus

My husband has wandered off down his own solitary path taking alcohol as his friend not me.

Energy or Lack of it

Take a moment to think when you feel energetic and when you don't.
The alcoholic surrounds himself with negative energy. He is often depressed, in poor spirits, thinks the world is against him and no one understands him. He exudes negativity.
The constant need to put up a front/a façade against the world drains energy. Any behavior that goes against your principles drains energy.
Every time you react to the actions of the alcoholic you lose energy. They drain us of our energy by their addictive presence. They crush our spirit.

Isolation

By the sheer nature of the problem, partners of alcoholics are isolated.
They are ashamed and embarrassed, confused and doubtful. They wrongly blame themselves. As if they aren't doing enough, or haven't yet found the correct solution.

You don't know what to do, that you haven't done previously, and you don't know who to talk to.
The alcoholic needs you to feel this way, to feed his dominance, his control and his power.
By not telling anyone. By keeping quiet. By making excuses. By refusing invitations, you are unwittingly and unknowingly condoning the behavior.
Any behavior that covers up an alcoholic's actions condones the behavior.
-By ringing in sick after a heavy drinking session.
-Cleaning up after him
-Allowing mental abuse

-Allowing physical abuse
-Driving him around when he is drunk
-Letting him drive when he insists he is sober and you know he is not.
-Topping up the credit card and mortgage payments

During this time partners are isolated. The alcoholic needs you to be. Not everyone wants to go to counseling or AL Anon meetings, let alone to admit to themselves that the problem has got this bad.

It takes a long time to sink in, that the more this secret is upheld, the longer the problem will go on.

The alcoholic will continue to have the time of his life while you continue to cook, clean, cosset and condone.
But there is hope and you, the partner of an alcoholic have choices, although you just don't know it yet.

Detox Units and Hospitals

A month before Christmas six years ago my husband's drinking became so bad that he was admitted to a detox unit for ten days.
There was no visiting, only one phone call a day after four days.

What sheer bliss.
An enforced holiday away from that horrible behavior.
I felt as though I had been given a ten day vacation. What a feeling of freedom. He was being cared for by experts and for a few days I did not have to put up with the drunken antics and verbal abuse.

But life goes on and his place of employment needed to be told. I fronted up to them on the Monday morning.
They were literally gob smacked. − What this wonderful employee? This great person who we have worked with for years, known so well and thought the world of?
Was I sure??
We knew he drank a bit − but!!!
We had no idea!
Why hadn't I said something?
What could they do to help?

When is a Good Time to Admit the Problem?

There is never a good time to come out and say - "You know I have this problem. I live with an alcoholic who is making my life miserable. I'm scared, confused and I don't know what to do."

Birthdays, Christmas, weekdays, tomorrow, last week – when do you say this? Who do you say it to? Do you just drop a hint after discussing the weather?

You also remember the few times you have broached the subject before and you have been met with disbelief and astonishment.

Believe me it is not simple. None of this is simple but after dealing with it logically it becomes easier.

After a stay in a detox unit people do begin to change their minds. It doesn't matter now what they think, but suddenly they start saying things like –"Well it must be worse than we thought."

But they hadn't thought because they didn't know anything about it. People say silly things.

My husband was horrified that he was being medicated in a secure detox unit. How had it come to this?

Antabuse

After ten days he came home.

Released with Antabuse tablets for six months. This medication makes the drinker very ill if they consume any alcohol.

But he was never going to drink again – he couldn't believe that over time he got that bad.

He was also to attend AA meetings and take several weeks off work.

This was the best Christmas we had had in years. Hope started to creep back in. May be this time.

He couldn't believe that some people who had been in the unit with him, had been there three or four times. Many were professional people like him. Wouldn't you think they would learn - he said?

Initially he promised to take the Antabuse tablets every morning in front of me to prove that yes he was in fact taking them. This lasted a few months and he decided he didn't need them any more as he had learnt a valuable lesson.

Cancer

Early the following year he became ill and no one could find out what was wrong with him. Being a drinker, everything relating to alcohol induced diseases was tested to no avail.

Eventually biopsies were done and stage four Hodgkin's disease was diagnosed. A cancer of the bone marrow: stage one being very curable, stage four not so.

No one ever doubted he would not survive. Our youngest granddaughter was twelve months old and he was going to see her go to school and that was all there was to it.

Chemotherapy began and ended successfully six months later.

A month into the chemotherapy the specialist threatened to stop the treatment and give it to a more deserving patient who desperately wanted to live and not one who was trying to kill himself with alcohol.

My husband was horrified. How dare they even think of stopping his treatment?

Three years later he was in total remission.

Cleared of stage four Hodgkin's. The specialist was amazed.

The drinking continued. Two more stays in secure detox units followed.

Obligation

We have been conditioned during our lives to help. To care for and nurture someone who is ill. To do whatever you can to assist and get that person back on the road to recovery.
We believe this is what is expected of us. But for how long?
And even when the person we are supposedly caring for doesn't want or think they need help.
I married this person thirty four years ago. When my granddaughter thinks dinosaurs roamed the earth.
For better or worse etc etc. This was a good partnership once. We were in his words, "a team."
But somewhere along the way without our noticing it, that partnership became very lopsided.

Somehow I got bound up in the wrongful knowledge that because of the contract I had entered into, I alone was responsible for getting him all the help he needed.
By whatever means.

Even though we are hardly ever happy or rarely laugh and smile with this person, we feel obliged to stay.

In doing so, we make ourselves miserable and in turn the alcoholic merrily goes on doing what they want.
Not drinking any less, nor worrying at all about how their family feels.
In fact they care less and less about their own and other people's feelings, never giving them a thought.
They hurt the ones closest to them and still we feel obligated to stay.
In this pursuit we completely lose sight of the fact that we were not put on this earth to be solely responsible for another human being.

No one can be responsible for the actions or thoughts of another adult person.

No one, not even a wife or a partner.

Until you acknowledge this important fact you cannot begin to see any way out of the problem.

Conversation becomes a thing of the past as the alcoholic drinks more and more, barreling through life with a tunnel vision mentality, doing whatever he likes. The partner becomes a mere side issue, rather like an annoying bug. The alcoholic couldn't care less about anyone but himself.

AA will say this is the disease manifesting itself and not the person. More a little later about the "disease", but this problem is a major part of the person and I am unable to separate the two.

And still we feel obligated to stay and try to change them.

They Must be Responsible

They have made their choice and must in turn be responsible for the consequences of their actions. They must ultimately be responsible for themselves.

This lesson I am afraid is learnt by us the partners, very very slowly.

I thought my husband needed me to stay with him, that he would maybe die if I didn't and it would be my fault.

Once again another slow lesson learnt.

He survives without me. He copes. He hasn't died. And if he did die from two bottles of vodka in twenty four hours that is his choice. His responsibility. His life.

It is not my life's mission to keep him alive.

I cannot be responsible for how another human being chooses to live - or die. I can only be responsible for myself. My obligation is to myself alone.

What Will They Think?

We have heard that alcoholism is an illness, so once again we feel obligated to stay and help this sick person.

Ask yourself right now – "How much has your help been till now?"
If I was a gambling person I'd be betting that you answer would be – NONE.

We are concerned about what "They" will think.

What will our families think, the neighbors, and our work colleagues?
We are conditioned to think that the great hordes of folk that make up the "They" in our minds are judging us.
In time you will see that this exists only in your own thoughts, because you are mentally trying to hold up a picture and act a life that is not true.
If that doesn't make much sense at the moment, ask yourself. Even if they are judging you – so what?
A later chapter deals with change and choices at many levels. To change you must find and abide by your inner most values.
Your morals. Your truthful intuition.
What you know deep down to be right for you. When you have understood this and put it into practice, it will not matter one iota, what anyone else thinks.

He was standing there, but a stranger now inhabited his body. A stranger who swore and cursed and drank for days on end. Not caring if I was in the house, out of town or on Mars.

Even with the mental abuse (and often though not in my case – physical abuse) I stayed.

It is devastating to your soul to see someone you love destroying themselves, ever so slowly.

Slow suicide by alcohol.

But the bottom line is – you can't do anything about it. Except to let them go to it. Give them free reign. They will sink or swim. This is very hard to get your head around.

It takes a long time to realize that they will drink no matter what you do. This is extremely difficult to comprehend but it is absolutely true.

Unless they feel the need to change, nothing you or anyone else does will change them.

Nothing.

Acting a Part

Alcoholics thrive on acting up. It feeds their souls, and makes them feel better and justifies what they are doing.

They love an audience. A controllable audience of only one or two is preferable.

So they act up and we react. Over and over again.

Remove the audience participation and things start to change. It is a little bit like a child having a tantrum.

Leave the house and go next door for a while and it becomes – 'I look a bit silly here having this hissy fit with no one watching. Not quite the same but you get the picture. You don't have to sit in the best seats watching the performance or waiting for acts two, three and four to begin. If you had paid to watch the performance and didn't like the acting, or found the theme distasteful, you would not hesitate to grab your bag and leave.

Not All the Answers

I don't have all the answers to the problem that you are now facing. No one does. Because every one of us has slightly different problems. But you will begin to question, to realize that there is a light at the end of the tunnel. Life can get better than this.
Every woman I have spoken to who has left an alcoholic husband **always** says the same thing.

"I got to a point where I thought – there must be more to life than this."

Every one of them has said the same thing.
Without any prompting whatsoever.

You must ask yourself the same question.

- Is this the life you want?

- Is this the life you want in five years time?

- Is this as good as it gets?

- Do I deserve better?

Is This As Good As It Gets?

When the only time you have peace of mind is when your husband is away, at work, or in hospital, something is definitely not right. I would often get up when my husband had gone to sleep. I loved the peace and quiet. But this isn't right. It can't go on like this, but you can't see how to stop it. Unfortunately the answer is it won't get any better.
You keep on hoping that the next counseling session or hospital stay will make him see sense.
It all comes back to the same solution.

Nothing will change unless you do.

The alcoholic is not going to change – not yet.
He is content at the moment. What reason has he got to change? He is fed, clean clothes are provided, the image he projects to the outside world is in tact and he can drink as much as he wants. The partner tops up the credit card or adds money to the bank account, should he overspend.
He thinks his wife is overreacting to his drinking.
The "You don't know when you are well off" and "I'm not doing you any harm" mentality kicks in. They make out that you alone are the big bad wolf. Doubt creeps in again. Perhaps it is me. I had better shut up.

Video Rewind

At this point do an imaginary video rewind of your past few years. What was your life like two years, five years, ten years ago? What would you have thought if back then, you could have seen how it is now?
Truthfully

How are the finances? Have they improved?
Are they going backwards?

Slow Realization

You never wanted this day to come, could never in a hundred years imagine it would arrive.
The day when enough is enough.
Deep down you know that things aren't getting any better.
In fact they are getting worse, a lot worse.
You can see no way that your life will improve if your partner continues on the same path as the last few years.

It is a terrible plummeting realization. You know deep down that something has to be done. You can't look back in two years time and say I did nothing and the situation hasn't changed. You know that unless you do something it will just carry on and on and on.
You will continue to be miserable, the alcoholic will continue on – same old, same old.

This realization to make some sort of change is not an overnight decision. It has been formed over months, sometimes years of toing and froing thoughts.

This person who you thought you would spend a lifetime with has made it impossible to do.
Nothing you say or do can make them see that.
And one day it arrives.

The day when enough is enough!

First Small Steps

The whole dilemma of alcohol addiction, throws the marriage into disarray over time.
The feelings for the partner are slowly eroded with every bad drinking episode.
Trust, sympathy, kindness, respect, loyalty and love get slowly, slowly worn away.
They trample all over them.

I am unable to separate the drunk, unreasonable man who is unable to stand, can't focus and who is yelling obscenities, from the man who twelve hours later wants forgiveness and love because he is sorry and will never do it again.

This to me is the same person, but if you can feel the same for both Dr Jekyll and Mr Hyde – good luck.
The time has come to draw some lines in the sand. Whether you stay with the alcoholic or leave some new rules need to be laid down – by you.
This is the first small step in the journey of change.

Beginning to Change

When we are in the middle of a bad situation that is encompassing our daily lives, it is helpful to step away from the problem for a short time. Remove yourself if possible to look at the dilemma from afar.
When we are inside it, it is all encompassing and overwhelming.
Remember alcoholics try control, confuse, intimidate, befuddle, irrationalize and threaten on purpose. They are masters at it.

Try to get a time when you can look in at the problem. Imagine it as looking in a window at the dilemma.

Remember the moment, whatever the bad moment was, the horrible scene that was playing out when you thought - "Enough is enough. I can't go on like this. There must be more to life than this." Keep this memory stored in a little mental box labeled (E is E) because you will need it later.

Contentment

I don't believe we can aspire to always have great happiness. Otherwise we would constantly be walking about with a large silly grin all over our faces.

Just as we do not always have great sadness. The trick is to strive for the middle ground of contentment.

To be content with what we have and what we have achieved. To be comfortable in our own skin.

We now have to find how to get to that middle ground.

To do this you have to listen to your instincts, your inner voice which sets the values that you uphold, your gut feeling if you want to call it that. Your "Doing it because it feels right" instinct.

Learn to act more and more on these feelings.

You need to weed out all the comments from well meaning people. Weed out all the advice from the outside world. Maybe they mean well, but they are not in your predicament.

They are their thoughts and ideas – not yours.

These people have not walked a mile in your moccasins. You have to listen to your inner voice, your gut feeling. And to do that you need to ask yourself soul searching questions to get to your own personal inner truth.

Questions

- Is this what I want?
- Do I like my life now?
- Can my partner provide the life I want?
- Do I want to carry on this way for another year?
- Is this behavior that I putting up with right?
- Do I deserve better?
- Would I rather live in a one bedroom flat than where I am now?
- If I had an hour to get out what would I take?
- Did this answer surprise me?
- Who will care for me if I don't?
- What will happen if I do nothing?
- What have I done so far that has made anything better?
- If my partner died tonight how would I feel?

Answering questions that are directed at your soul, your intuition, your inner self, is the only way to get to the core truth of your values.
Listen to what your true feelings are telling you.
If it feels wrong you are in fact going away from/going against your values.

What is really true for you? Best for you. Be true to yourself with your answers. No excuses. It is all about you. We need to be comfortable and respect ourselves.
Do you respect yourself now?
We need to stand up for our values. Our beliefs. Learn to search for the answers more and more by listening to those true feelings.

Don't do things because others think you should. Or because you feel obligated or because it is what's expected. Do it because you know it is in line with your true beliefs, your values.

Keep Seeking the Truth

Keep asking yourself questions and always seek truthful answers. Not other people's answers. They won't be what are true to you.

Deep down we all have our own personal inner values. We set our standards and live our lives by this benchmark in our minds. Trying to continually live against our values slowly makes us ill. Even in the smallest way, use these values as a guide. Always listen to what your gut feeling is trying to tell you. Each time you use this method of self examination you will become stronger in your own self belief. You will slowly build your confidence up bit by bit.
Confidence builds confidence which in turn builds self esteem.

We always have these values to fall back on. They are the principals of our belief system and will never let you down.

If you find you answer a question with an "I don't know", that is not good enough. Think about it and answer truthfully. What is really true for you?

You may get some surprising answers and not what you really expected.

Of course it is not always easy.

We are programmed not to think in the first instance of what is best for 'me'.
We as wives, mothers and partners put others first. Always.

How often do you say 'Yes' to something when deep down you are kicking yourself for saying it because you really wanted to say 'No'.

Listen to the voice that is being sent to your brain – Why the hell did you say yes, when every truthful feeling was saying no. Slow down a bit. Take time to listen to yourself. Don't blurt out the first thing on your tongue.
Of course all this takes a bit of effort and soul searching. But what have you got to lose?
It really depends on how much you want the situation to change.

Change

Change means doing something. Acting on your discoveries. Some people aren't willing to do this. So they stay where they are - miserable. It is a choice. Everything is a choice.

There is a way out, but only you have the capabilities that you have found inside yourself to make the changes happen. To act.
We can read for ever about what we need to do to change our lives, our jobs, our weight, our outlook. All the reading in the world will do nothing unless you *act*.
Your self knowledge will show you the way.
Of course everything will not be crystal clear immediately.

But you have begun. In time with honest answers to searching questions an inner truth will surface. It may be frightening at first, scary to achieve, but ultimately you will know what has to be done.

The way your life is at the moment is not right – or you would not still be reading this book.

These truthful answers slowly lead to what it is you need to do. Some semblance of logical thought begins to emerge. The clutter starts to clear from your mind and now you have direction. A direction to put changes in place, to improve the life you have.

No More

When you make a stand and say 'No more, I can't live like this', the façade starts to crumble.

You are giving the alcoholic back full responsibility for his own life.

There is no more hiding and deceiving, pretence or dominance and the control the alcoholic had, starts to disappear. The alcoholic thinks he can fool all of the people all of the time - he can't.

He only succeeds in fooling himself.

I can't reiterate enough how this truthful questioning of your values can achieve results. Answers we may not be able to put in place immediately. But we suddenly see that we have the means to put a plan in place. Ultimately you need to stand up for what you feel and therefore know to be right.

Feel good about the decisions you have made.

Don't apologize or back down.

Take pride in your values. Be true to yourself.

More on Values

Dictionary definition: – One's principles or standards, one's judgment of what is important in life.

Values are your inner feelings that set a benchmark as to where you see right and wrong.
We all decide what our individual values are.

Are we honest, kind, giving, truthful or law abiding.
These things are important to us and we live our lives around these principles. No one tells us or forces these values on to us, and in turn we realize that we cannot force our values on to anyone else.
We cannot change others. But we *can* change ourselves.
The realization will occur that the alcoholic is in fact going against our principles, our values.
The way you are being treated, how you have to live, the whole horrible situation is going against your values.

Enough is Enough. This behavior is not acceptable to me.

This line has become one that I have repeated many times.
It stands me in good stead. When I say it I know I am right.
You may not have any control over what anybody else does, but the magic key is that you do have control over how you respond to what they do.

Sometimes it is time to say – enough. I deserve better than this. Get off the merry-go-round.

Accept - yes this bad thing is happening but I don't have to participate anymore.
I can leave.

Detachment

To me, to be able to detach emotionally, to look after yourself, to get on with your life, to take time to heal and let the alcoholic be entirely responsible for his own life, is a breakdown of the marriage.

Because I can't separate the person and the antics of the alcoholic, I find detachment within marriage to be unfathomable.
If you detach physically and emotionally - if the alcoholic becomes too bad this happens as a matter of course – and to me even if you are living in the same house the marriage has already broken down.

You might as well be flatting and just sharing expenses. If your flat mate behaved like the drinker in your life you would most likely throw them out.
Everyone to their own. This book is my personal account entirely. But detach you must for your own sanity.
Give the alcoholic back total responsibility for their actions.

To Leave or to Stay

Ultimately I believe that the alcoholic has to be left.
I don't mean they have to be left for good, but for a while at least.

Sometimes the fact that they are alone jolts them into seeing the problem that has been created, in a new light.
The fact that they thought that this would never happen – 'She will never leave me, she knows when she is well off' isn't cutting it any more.

Suddenly no marriage, no friend, no housekeeper, no company, no cook, no conversation, no audience, no support. This hopefully will be the wake up call they need.

If in time they can put plans in place to concertedly get help – not just promise to do this and do nothing. But literally make changes to themselves and their pattern of life; this may be a turning point.
"Well done" is better than "well said."
But don't expect miracles. They are thin on the ground.

The alcoholic is a master at promising, and apologizing over and over again. They are experts.
This does not make it right; neither does it go any way to getting help for their problem.
All it does is support a delaying tactic. They often have very important things to attend to before they can deal with their addiction.

Only when results have been achieved – drinking has stopped, proof that bank balances are not being raided weekly and a concerted attempt to live without any addictions, should any thought be given to returning.
I say any addictions because at this point the alcoholic will often transfer or replace the alcohol, with gambling or spending up large at the shops every day.

Leaving is difficult, traumatic and scary.
But so is staying.

Communication

I don't mean that the alcoholic should be left without communication. If communication is lost all is lost.
Talking sensibly about the problem that alcohol has created, means dialogue cannot be entered into if alcohol is present.
Make that one simple rule. Any alcohol - no communication.
You be the judge. You know when he has been drinking.

Maybe this won't happen for quite a while. There will be problems but you need to stick to your rule.
Stick to your principles.
You know very well that communication with anyone who is drunk is useless. So don't even think about it until they are sober. I successfully sorted out money, house and property with good legal assistance and still talk to my husband. But only when he is sober.

The Two Choices

As I have said before, the answers are not laid out carefully in this book of mine. Only choices, options and what I have found out along the way.
You have got to make up your own mind based on your own personal circumstances and your new found values.
If you feel confident with how your partner has acted regarding changing, you must be your own judge. You alone have to live your life.
Whatever happens, this above all else. You must let *them* make their own decisions about what they will do. It is all up to them.
You have given them back total control and responsibility for their own lives.

If they want to do nothing about it – so be it.
Once again it must be their choice alone.
They are grown adults.

This is easier to read than to do.
I never said it was easy. Every day there will be doubts and uncertainties, distress and fear.
Although you had all that when you lived with him.
Now there is an opportunity for him to heal this large crack that has developed in the relationship. An opportunity for him to make things better.

There is always hope. We must never ever lose it. The alcoholic may turn his life around, get professional help, look at his choices, change the environment that sets off the triggers, redesign his life and offer a better future for you both.
Or he can continue to drink.
These are the only two choices out there and this time apart will go some way to providing an answer.

To Return or Not

If you are happy to return – do so.
Just do one thing before you return.
Go back to the (E is E) box that you filed away in the memory bank. Open it and remember.
If you are not happy to return - don't.
Only you know the answer. It is your choice. Your life.
No cajoling, begging, bargaining, brainwashing or blackmail.
You are the only one who knows how you feel.
Listen to your values, your gut reaction, your inner voice, your true self.
Act on this. No one else has to live your life.

No one knows what you put up with before you left.
It was bad enough to leave.
Is it good enough to return?

Will He Die Without Me?

More likely than not drinking sessions will continue after you have left. I find that these need to be reported.
The audience mentality is still there so the alcoholic needs to let others know that he is drinking for whatever reason.

You have to accept this as fact, and answer along the lines of
–'Ok if that's what you want to do'
Don't be taken in by threats or blackmail.
Keep referring to your standard answer.
Always, always remember that you are not responsible for another person's life or death.

My Clear Conscious

I can look in the mirror and categorically say that I have done whatever I knew possible at the time, to find doctors, social workers, psychiatrists, psychologists, counselors and specialists. Nothing 'helped'.

My husband continues to drink.

Days go by. Is he alive or dead? Has he had a stroke? Has he fallen down the stairs? Is he driving? Has he been arrested?
It is not my responsibility how he lives his life.
Let him lead it.
He may get arrested. He may have to appear in court. Let the process unfold naturally.
Leave well alone.

Maybe he will become so drunk that he can't go out and buy more alcohol. After a few days he will most likely sober up. Let him face the consequences of his actions.
On the other hand this could be the wake up call he needs. He has to find his own help. He can use a phone. You know that. What is the worst that can happen?
He will die.
He chose to die that way.
It is a tough love situation. Tough on both sides.
But it was tough before wasn't it?

Whether They Change or Not

Whether they change or not, is not the question now.

For your own sanity, your own peace of mind, you need to keep yourself removed from the problem for the present and put your thoughts and health in order.
You will be no good to anyone – yourself or your family if you are unwell. An enforced break from this person will be scary, but it will also bring relief, clarity and time to think.
Don't rush. Don't rush to do anything. Take time.

Keep reminding yourself why you left. You could no longer live in that world. The behavior was unacceptable.

You don't have the answers for the alcoholic, but you have the means to make a change in yourself and your attitude.

Look after yourself.
The alcoholic also has to look after himself, or not, as he chooses.
He is an adult who can choose to do with his life what he wants.

'Yes I have a Problem'

When things have got to the stage of detox and hospital admissions, the alcoholic may be forced to see that yes he may have some sort of problem.

It is still unfathomable to them that they are responsible for this problem. It must be someone else's fault.
They may arrive at the conclusion that they are partly responsible and even go so far as to say "Yes I have a problem."
But beware.
The next response to doctors is "Ok I have this problem – There I have said it. Now you fix me. You with all the qualifications and the answers – you fix me."
This unfortunately is still denial. They still do not realize that they personally have to be responsible for what they do.
Are the doctors hearing 'Yes I have a problem. What can *I* do about it?' No.

Individual Responsibility

It all comes back to the only one who can do anything to implement change is the individual.
Many people can put forward all sorts of suggestions for help. Group sessions, books, AA and therapy. Medical help can assist with the medical conditions that arise from the consumption of too much alcohol.

Lots of people are willing to assist, but if the alcoholic is just going through the motions, telling the counselors what they think they want to hear and not really getting to the core of the 'change yourself' the inevitable will occur.

All the medical brains in the world can do nothing if the individual does not want to stop drinking.

Alcoholics are not Fools

These drinkers are not fools. They are intelligent people who hold down responsible, corporate positions.
They are often in a position of telling others what to do, are in charge of large numbers of staff, deadline driven, high powered decision makers, planners, often in jobs of leadership.

They don't like being questioned and told there may be another side to their coin. They don't like looking inside themselves. Let alone having some stranger looking at that inner person.
So they put up a 'front', an act for the outside world.
Theirs employers, their staff, their friends, their doctor, or members of the family who are not close.

They have all these people fooled – or so they think – as well as themselves. And when in accepting that they might have a problem, they really have convinced themselves that by saying that, it might just be enough to shut up the immediate family for a while.

Maintaining the Façade

They become convinced that their problem is not as bad as any one else in the hospital or at the meeting. The ' I'm not as bad as them ' mentality kicks in because the façade that they are so vigorously holding up to the world is in tact – for the moment.

As long as they are able to maintain a semblance of normality with this front they will not admit their problem is really that bad.

As long as the balls can all be kept in the air, they can pay their way, not really doing any harm (in their eyes) and are not really being a bad individual, they will still be in denial.

They can't honestly change while holding on to this denial. They don't want to; because they can't see that they are doing any wrong along the way. They don't want to change a life that they are happy with.

That is the question. Do they really want to change?

Change means finding answers and **acting** on those answers. Moving out of their comfort zone.

Is this just a bit too hard?

Change means honest self examination.

A new person can never hope to emerge when denial is still a big part of the picture. They may on the other hand want to change. Though only if someone else tells them how and it involves nothing that they don't want to do.

Alcoholics Anonymous

As previously stated this entire book is written from my own personal experiences and thoughts.

Arrived at after living with a heavy drinker who became a chronic alcoholic.

This chapter is no different.

In no way have I ever, or ever will, make light of the problem of addiction.

This book has been written from my personal perspective only.

What I have seen and lived through. What I have seen my husband go through.

When my husband went to the first counseling session attended by about ten people he was told that only one or two people in the room would improve. But would never be cured. He came home and said 'Well there's not much hope really is there?'
Not a very positive start.

As we all know the 12 steps of AA are the backbone of their system.

Step 1 – We admitted we were powerless over alcohol – that our lives had become unmanageable.

Step 2 – Came to believe that a Power greater than ourselves could restore us to sanity.

Step 3 – Made a decision to turn our will over to God as we understand him.
The alcoholic is told that they are completely powerless over alcohol, which I take to mean they have no control where alcohol is concerned.
They have control to do everything else in their life, hold down jobs, travel overseas, run companies and drive cars.

They are also told that this is a disease, an illness, which they have no control over.
This illness that can only be bought under control one day at a time by going to AA meetings and talking with people who have similar problems. This husband of mine goes to an AA meeting – this man who does not have a religious or spiritual bone in his body is confronted with these facts.

47

And told that the third step is to turn his life over to God as he understands him, to restore his sanity. I personally think that these ideas do nothing to encourage hope, and must surely add to the torment already rampant in the alcoholic's body. I would find this demoralizing and unfathomable. I would flop back in my chair and think there was nothing I could do – I am sick and all they can do is talk to me. Talk me out of being sick.

And I will never be cured. I will always be ill.

Surely these 'facts' of illness and a higher power restoring health, take all the responsibility away from the individual.

They may not be in control, but to throw the problem out into the great abyss must seem horrifyingly scary and frightening, let alone incomprehensible and unrealistic, to the already troubled alcoholic.

We must all be responsible for our own actions.

We can all make choices to change.

Not for one second am I saying conquering addiction is easy.

I am merely saying that I have trouble with turning responsibility over to God as we know him, alone.

Our God

God as we understand him or a Higher Power is just too vague and incomprehensible for some people.

Whether we believe in a God as a superhuman being, a majestical spiritual force or perhaps we don't believe in a God at all, the alcoholic can't wait around for God to help.

What help has this God/this Higher Power been so far?

The alcoholic must act himself. When he is ready.

He is responsible for himself and his choices.

We are all individually responsible for ourselves.

I have been saying all along that change will not happen until you, yourself make it happen.
I believe this applies to the alcoholic as well.

I believe the change must come from within.

This is difficult for a person with an alcohol addiction, as they do not like themselves. They don't want to 'look' at themselves. They think it is wimpy and very uncool. Only for weird people who hug trees. They do not want to ask questions of their true feelings.
Nor do they want to face the truthful answers.

The True Personality

The alcoholic is so busy maintaining the façade that they think needs to be kept in place, the true person is in time so suppressed that they almost disappear.
So change for the alcoholic, I believe, is doubly difficult because the true person needs to be uncovered.
They deny the existence of their true self because they think it is too difficult, too painful, too hard to confront.

They are constantly 'running away' from their true self who they do not like.
They become a hamster on a wheel of their own making, wearing a blindfold.
Alcohol has a louder voice than their own true feelings.

Al Anon

Al Anon meetings are to help people who live with alcoholics.

Once again the 12 step programme comes into play and it can be very helpful coming to grips with the first step. Once you can see that you personally have no control over another person's drinking, no matter what you do they won't stop, this is a step in the right direction.

Then we come up against step 2 and 3.

I can accept that the problem has happened and that I have no control over what someone else does.

But I do have control and can choose what I do.

I can't throw my problem out into the unknown realms of uncertainty in the hopes that somehow it will come right.
It is up to me. We are all responsible for ourselves.
Having said that, this is my opinion only.
If Al Anon helps you that is good. Everyone is different.

It would be a perfect world if those we loved, lived as we would prefer them to live.
This will never happen.
You cannot mould someone else into your way of thinking.
The sooner you come to terms with this the better off you will be.

Al Anon presents the 12 steps and offers experience gained by others and comfort. They do not lead or offer opinions.

Let Go and Let God

This line crops up a lot around addictions.

In the middle of the worst time with an alcoholic these words sound insane. We, the partners are hanging on for all we are worth. Trying to get this partner of ours to see logic, to see the damage that they are creating to the family, to us and to themselves. Why the heck would we just let him go?

So we keep on trying, keep trying to control him, to control the way he lives. We don't know it at the time, but we are trying to do the impossible. We think that if only we can control what he does he will improve.

We keep trying and trying to no avail. We have got to keep on trying to maintain control because what will happen if we don't? As the problem escalates we try more and more to change them, all the time getting ourselves deeper and deeper into an impossible situation.

Eventually we realize that we can't control him, we never could, so the only answer is **we** must change. We must stand back and let whatever happens happen.
Another way of saying let go and let God.

Maybe this is the wake up call he needs.

The alcoholic is suddenly – oops – responsible for everything he does.

We can do nothing more.
Maybe bad things will happen. So be it.
We can do nothing about it.

This person is an adult. He knows right from wrong.

He can make his own choices in life.

He will sink or swim. We can only hope.

A year after I left my husband and home of thirty four years he was convicted of excess alcohol while driving. He was fined and lost his licence for six months. By the time he was able to drive again he was no longer able to work and the house had to be sold.

You can't dictate which way the scales will tip.

I wish things had turned out differently, but that hasn't happened. It saddens me that he is still living his own version of 'Groundhog Day.'

Wishing and hoping things had turned out differently, is a very effective way to waste time and achieves nothing.

The past is always part of us, but it must stay right there where it belongs – in the past. We have lived through it to get where we are today. So leave it where it belongs.

Accept and Learn

Accept that it has happened, learn from it, but don't keep regurgitating it.

The past can never be changed. What people did and said, didn't do or didn't say, can never be changed.

Don't waste the life you have now, dwelling on the past.

Strive to do better.

Live in the present.

Be thankful for what you have now. Be grateful for supportive family and friends.

Be grateful for all that is important to you.

Illness, Sickness or Disease

This is a hard one and we all have our own opinions. This book has been written entirely from my own point of view and continues that way. I am no doctor and never will be.

Is an addiction to alcohol an illness or not?
Is it inherited, in the genes? Do these people have different chromosomes than other people?
I feel the disease concept lets the alcoholic off the hook. It takes the responsibility off the alcoholic's shoulders.
One more thing that they can say – "It's not my fault – I have just got a disease and I can't help it."

I have no idea and few professionals seem to have the answers, but ultimately it doesn't matter. Being explained as an illness or not, what matters is how their actions are affecting our lives and what you are going to do about it.

It gets too difficult to live with day after day. It is not our mission in life to put up with mental and verbal abuse constantly. The great lows of a depressed alcoholic, the cruel antics of the drunken person. The windscreen wiper effect, of two personalities.
It all gets too much.
There must be a life out there better than this.
This is not being loved by someone.
Loving people do not act this way.

You have got to look after yourself.

If it is an illness, it will be along time before an anti alcohol pill comes along. Are you going to wait for it?

If it is hereditary or in the genes you can do nothing to change that.

You personally can do nothing to change the alcoholic. They must want to change themselves.

Cancer and Diabetes

We have diseases such as cancer and diabetes. Is alcohol a disease like that?

My husband wasn't an alcoholic twenty years ago. A person becomes diseased by alcohol after consuming large quantities over a long period of time. Many illnesses arise from the excess consumption of alcohol.

Why are alcoholics only treated by talking to them? We don't treat the cancer patient or the diabetic this way.

Or the person addicted to nicotine.

About now several people will be throwing their hands in the air in horror. That's fine. They are as entitled to their own opinions.

Once man thought the world was flat.

Perhaps we are treating alcoholics the wrong way. I wish I had the answer to help these miserable souls. The symptoms of alcoholism only manifest themselves after the person has consumed the alcohol. If the person doesn't drink the alcohol the symptoms don't appear.

Compare this to cancer or diabetes.

The drinker can choose when the symptoms appear. The cancer patient doesn't. Is cigarette smoking a disease as well? Is alcohol addiction the result of a chemical deficiency? Which in turn causes physical diseases when the body reacts to the excessive consumption of the poison

found in the alcohol?
I don't think I will live long enough to find out.

A Tangled Mess

I believe that the alcoholic desperately wants to change. But only if he doesn't have to implement the change.

As time goes on they live with great mental torment wanting desperately not to be the person they are.
But at the same time frantically avoiding any personal change for fear of losing the imaginary control they so wrongly believe they have.
With their need to somehow punish themselves, their self dislike and their lack of self esteem, they talk themselves into becoming victims.
They become the ultimate pessimist ending up demoralized by negativity. This blanket of negativity keeps them safe and protected from having to take any positive action; to initiate any change.

They want to have peace of mind, to get off the treadmill that they are on, but they don't want to change themselves.
They want others to do it for them.
It is indeed a tangled mess.

A Foot in Each Camp

Alcohol addiction is a huge boiling pot of denial.
The alcoholic can reach a point when he knows there is a problem and he is out of control. He will even admit it.
Yes – I have this problem and I am out of control.

But deep deep down **he** doesn't want to fix it. He wants it fixed by someone else, anyone else but him. He may not be at all happy with the extent that the addiction has got him into trouble. But he still feels that if the problem (that he has admitted he has got) can once again be bought under control (as he sees it) he can carry on as before.

He still does not want to change enough. It is still too hard.

He is still convinced it is really not all his fault. The 'I'll only have two drinks a day to keep me steady' kicks in again. Once again he kids himself that by having a foot in each camp he is in control and not really causing too much harm to the family

Warped denial.

The Wall of Denial

The wall of denial is hard to break down.

As more negative things occur the alcoholic needs to find more people to blame. The blame bolsters the evidence that their brain seeks to reiterate the fact that they are correct.

It is not their fault that they have this problem, everybody else has added their little bit to make their life a misery.

His father – *It is in the genes, what chance did I have?* Doctors and therapists add to this so it must be true – in his eyes.

His family's brick is the first in the wall of denial.

His job was very pressured. *-They should have seen the stress that I was under* – the employer's brick gets added.

That counselor said only 5% of us will improve. *What chance do I have?* – the counselors' brick.

The doctor says it is an illness and won't go away – the doctor's brick.

I've got to let God help. Why did he let this happen in the first place? – God's brick.

My employer kicked me when I was down.
(This is completely untrue. They tried to help him 100%)

But the employer gets another brick for good measure.

The family who try to say that he is hurting them as well as himself – the family brick.

And so it goes on, this wall of denial that he has constructed around himself. As I have said, some part of them desperately wants to change. But that change is too great to deal with. Because every time a problem arises in their life the answer is to be found at the bottom of a bottle.
The desire to want to initiate and continue with intimate personal change, that is mentally necessary, is just too hard. Or maybe they are not ready.

They Do Change

But change they do. They change inwardly, their spirits become deflated.
They can't see that the trap they are in is of their own making. They think everyone else has made it so.
They get angrier and angrier at their own behavior and so drink more and more to obliterate their problem, which in turn adds to the already extensive pile of trouble already created.

57

The hamster becomes more frantic with less and less common sense. By this time they have become ill. They have depression, poor appetite, erratic sleep patterns, poor concentration and lapses of memory. The illnesses now displayed are the outcome of constant bouts of heavy drinking.

Something to Avoid

In the process of coming back into control of your own life there are a few things to watch out for and avoid.

- Beware of people who think they have all the answers. They have no idea what your life was like before you left, but are always be willing to give you their 10 cents worth. They throw lines out there such as 'Someone must be able to help him?' or 'It really comes down to the family'.

It is like the death penalty. Lots of people agree with it but no individual person wants to be solely responsible.

The Trap

You have to keep in mind the "Straw that Broke the Camel's Back day".

That "Enough is Enough" box that you filed away mentally quite a while ago. One bad thing didn't happen that made you leave. It was slow, very slow, getting worse and worse.

Because they are now maybe sober, they can be charming, quite normal, as they seemed years ago and they want you back.

Why did I leave this person?

Once again let me say they are good actors. They put up a believable front to get what they want. But just under the surface is an angry person who thinks the world and his brother are against him, owes him something and no one understands.

As long as you have evidence of positive change you can decide what is best for you to do.

Only you know the answers.

Now – Not in the Future

The alcoholic thinks that things will be better some time in the future.

- When I have finished this job.

- When I sort myself out after this drinking episode.

- When winter is over.

- When I get this out of my system.

Always always in the future. The future that only exists in our imaginations.

When we are so fixed on some point in time that will never come, we completely lose sight of the **now.**

Thinking about being happy or having all our problems solved in the future will never happen.

None of us can live in the past or in the future. We can only live in the present. Now.

Make the most of now. Today.

Do the best we can for ourselves and our families today. Tomorrow exists only in our minds.

Years ago I copied these words into a notebook. I do not know who wrote these words but they are certainly appropriate to add to this page.

Those Two Days

There are two days in every week about which we should not worry, two days which should be kept from fear and apprehension.

One of those days is yesterday, with its mistakes and cares, its faults and blunders, its aches and pains. Yesterday has passed forever beyond our control. All the money in the world cannot bring back yesterday. We cannot undo a single act we performed. We cannot erase a single word we said. Yesterday has gone beyond recall.

The other day we should not worry about is tomorrow, with its possible adversities. Its burdens, its large promise and perhaps its poor performance.

Tomorrow is beyond our immediate control. Tomorrow's sun will rise, either in splendor or behind a mask of clouds, but it will rise. Until it does, we have no stake in tomorrow, for it is as yet unborn.

This leaves only one day – today.

Any man can fight the battles of just one day. It is only when you and I add the burden of those two awful eternities, yesterday and tomorrow, that we break down.

It is not the experience of today that drives men mad. It is the remorse or bitterness for something which happened yesterday or the dread tomorrow may bring. Let us therefore do our best to live but one day at a time.

Looking After Yourself

This journey that you are now setting out on has to be based on truth. By listening to your values, your conscious, your gut feeling, you already have the truthful answers that will stand you in good stead.
You cannot have better backup than your own true principles.

Even though you may initially start out alone you will very quickly meet kind people along the way. People who want to help. After what you have been through this feels a bit foreign at first, but accept their help and assistance gratefully. Everyone is not talking about you; they have enough problems of their own. They may stop for a few moments and say - 'Well goodness who would have thought it. What's for dinner?' Your problems are not important to other people.

Normally we don't need to change because we are happy with how things are. But when this everyday existence becomes unlivable and detrimental to our health we need to get out, change, and get our lives back into our control.
We fear change simply because we are stepping into the unknown. Why do we fear it?
More than likely it will be better.
So far whenever I have dipped my toe into unknown waters I have not had it nibbled, let alone bitten off.

The Heavy Lump of Dread

The lump of dread in your stomach, the tightening of muscles in the diaphragm and the heap of other problems caused by stress, slowly begin to subside. You have a direction and at last know where you are going.

It takes a while but with every step of achievement, confidence grows. Some mornings it may be hard to get motivated and get out of bed. Not every day will be a go forward, up and at it, sort of day.

On my way to work each day I pass a large residential facility for severely disabled people. They whiz along the footpath to the dairy strapped into their motorized wheelchairs. Mostly their only means of operating the chair is with a small lever that they operate with movement of their head. They have little control, if any, over their arms and legs.

 - Just get out of bed.

A Journal

About now is a good time to buy a journal. Not a diary – a diary is for dental appointments and such like. A book that you can use to jot things down. Anything you want to write down. Sentences from a book that have particular relevance. Some sayings just hit the nail on the head.

Perhaps the day hasn't gone so well. But most likely it has gone a lot better than you imagined. Write all the little things down. Dump words on the page. Don't go back and change anything. Leave it. Don't let anyone else read it. It is your own personal dumping ground.

In a year or so when you do go back and read those words you will be amazed at how far you have come and what you have achieve.

Be open to new suggestions. Surround yourself with positive people. Do you need a small holiday? Perhaps someone you know needs a house sitter for a few weeks.
Consider new ideas.

Professional People

There will be times when you need to seek the help of professional people. Solicitors, banking consultants etc.
Don't be intimidated by them. They are people with problems just like you. We are apprehensive because we most likely haven't done this sort of thing before and don't know what to expect.

Just start at the beginning. It is always the best place to start. Pick up the phone book. Make that first call. Arrange an initial appointment. The first introductory meeting with professional people often has no charge. Ask about this over the phone.
Go armed to any appointment with pen and paper and a written list of questions that you need answers to. Write down the answers if you feel happy doing it this way. Often when you are given heaps of information, you get in the car and have forgotten half the answers by the time you get home. Don't let these people embarrass or intimidate you. Don't be flummoxed by big fancy buzzwords.
Ask them to explain if there is anything that you don't understand. Keep asking.
If for some reason, your gut feeling is not entirely happy with this person, say thank you very much and go back to the phone book.
These people are offering a service. You don't have to buy it. Soon this will be one major step accomplished. Well done. Add that to your confidence bank.

Do the same with any other professionals you need help from along the way. Choose the person who can best help you at the bank – wherever. Step by step you will get there.

If ever in doubt go back to your values.

There may be quite a lot of things to arrange. But they don't all need to be done today. Make a list of essential 'To Do's.' The others things on the list can wait for now.

If six meters of firewood is delivered in the summer, you don't pick it up all a once and stack it in the woodshed. You stand back and look at it hoping that it will magically go away, but of course this doesn't happen. So you start by picking up one piece at a time. You put a few pieces away and back you go and do some more. Sometimes another person comes along and helps. After some time, not all in one day, you get the wood stacked away. Break down jobs into manageable do-able sections.

Your doctor can also be a great help in putting you onto organizations that will be of help.
Go and talk to him/her truthfully.
Draw your self up a simple honest budget. Get advice if necessary.

Declutter

Have a tidy out of all possessions. Not throwing everything out in a mad rage, but putting items that you haven't used for a while, into a box. Clothes, old bills, plates, makeup, all sorts – pack them away. In a year's time if you haven't needed to rummage in the box looking for anything, you most likely can do without it. Throw it away.

The more clutter we have in our everyday life – in the car, in the medicine cabinet, in kitchen drawers, on bookshelves, on desks, the more stress is created by this muddle.

Can you easily lay your hands on what you want or do you have to spend ages ferreting around to find it?

You have enough stress at present without adding to it. Declutter. Get some order. File papers away. Label boxes. Throw out old papers that are not needed away.

Simplify

Clutter and mess cause stress. – Simplify, simplify, simplify. Free up some time. Aim for blank spaces in your diary.

We will not be given a medal at the end of our life for being the one with the most clutter and stress in our diary.

Set small goals only. Sometimes the goals we set further add to our stress because they are so huge and loom before us like mountain ranges. We start to rush about madly trying to create the time to do all these things. - Simplify.

Too many goals, too many things to do, too many "yes's" and not enough "no's" cause stress. As you will see this journey collects good people along the way. It has its pot holes and its challenges but kind people are out there, willing to help in many ways.

When you have moments of doubt, look back over your shoulder at what you have achieved - 'Well done!' We have learnt that we can't change the world, we can't change our partners, spouses, adult sons and daughters, but we do have the power and control to change ourselves. We all have our own individual lives to lead and how we choose to do this is entirely up to us.

34 Years is a Long Time.

My husband always says that I know him better than he knows himself. After thirty four years maybe this is true. Whatever the answer is, it doesn't matter. We can only hope to know ourselves well enough to be content in our own skin. He may never know about this book and probably doesn't want to. He will most likely never read this: -

'In recent years your soul has been tormented. You think that everything and the actions of everyone are against you. This is not true. You can't be still long enough to realize that the problem is you. You are always in the egg beater syndrome of torment or running away from yourself in the hopes that you will escape your problems. You don't want to look at yourself nor have others look either.
I wish for you a life of peace and contentment, but I am unable to give this to you.
You have been a huge part of my life. I have known you since I was sixteen. You are the father of my only child and the grandfather of my two grand daughters. This is solid history and can't be lost.
It saddens me deeply that you have chosen to put alcohol before your family. A family who loved you and held you in high esteem.
What you thought was heaven has become a living hell.'

Books I have found useful.

'How to Get From Where You Are to Where You Want To Be'– Jack Canfield

'You'll See It When You Believe It' – Wayne Dyer

'Pulling Your Own Strings' – Wayne Dyer

'Love the Life You Live' – Anne Hartley

'Empowering Women' – Louise L Hay

'You have Choices' – Charles Donaghue

'What is Your Life's Work? – Bill Jensen

'Aspirations-8 Easy Steps to Coach Yourself' - Andrea Molloy

'Wise Up' – Lindsey Dawson

10 Rules to Break and 10 Rules to Make – Bill Quain

'Resilience' – Anne Deveson

'What Are You Waiting For' – Justin Herald

'How to Stop Worrying and Start Living' – Dale Carnegie

'Feel the Fear and Do It Anyway' – Susan Jeffers

'Downshifting' – Polly Ghuzi & Judy Jones

Future Help

The help required for the alcoholic in the future will be complex. As individually complex as they are themselves.
This help will take time and money. It will involve a holistic package of assistance, taking into account the person as a whole and not just the addicted module.
They need to be counseled as to what can be done initially to help with the current problems that the drinking has caused.

Often the things that we see as being minor problems become overwhelming and all consuming to them.
For a while they need to be shown a positive road with small tasks that can be accomplished calmly on a day to day basis.
Never too many things to be done too quickly.

The specialized help also needs to address the causes of the addiction and not just the symptoms. What has caused them initially to have the need to medicate themselves with addictive substances? What has caused the low self esteem that they so often seem to have?
Most will deny this, as they have fooled themselves for so long their memory has erased the initial cause.
Somewhere there is a reason that they needed to drink in the first place.
It has taken years to get where they are today, so it can not be expected that an answer will be found or the problem solved in one or two hourly sessions.
We must not continue to address only the symptoms and not the cause of the problem. If the symptoms only are targeted the problem will always be rumbling under the surface, waiting to erupt again, maybe in a different form.

These drinkers have got themselves into patterns of thought and behavior that need to be altered. Patterns that need to 'unlearnt' – to be broken, and replaced with new ideas and responses, so they have tools to use in new ways when problems arise. New ways need to be offered, taught and practiced to deal with their negative thoughts, emotions and stress.

They must be looked at individually and not lumped together with a label. A label that negates their self worth. They do not constantly need to be reminded of their faults. They are well aware of them. They need to be encouraged and helped to build self esteem.

In a way their personal program needs to be reset. Something has popped them off their tracks. Illness and disease happen when things are out of balance in the body. This has happened to our addicts of alcohol.

A recent study in the United States has found that alcoholics have an uneven balance between two brain chemicals – glutamate and GABA. Addicts have an excess of glutamate, which enhances the desire for drugs and alcohol; GABA inhibits it, so restoring the balance reduces cravings. Much more research needs to be done but as I write it is progressing.

We must also look at changing the patterns of putting these addicts in detox units for seven days and then tossing them out. Some go straight to their families. Some go to half way houses and others go straight back where they came from.

Families have to carry on doing the day to day living that needs to be done and are ill equipped to look after a disturbed person who has just come from seven days detoxing. The families do not know what to do and are given little help. All they know is that their loved one must attend

counseling sessions or AA meetings. They begin to feel inadequate and watch the alcoholic like a hawk wondering what will happen next.
They do not know what to do to help.

Somehow the way we 'help' the alcoholic must change.
With alcohol so readily available and being the 'legal' drug of choice I feel we are in for an avalanche of problems in the near future.

AA is not for Everyone

My husband didn't believe in a God and couldn't understand the concept of a 'Higher Power'. AA was unable to help him. When someone tried to tell him that his 'Higher Power could be a bird or a butterfly he was flummoxed.
AA works for many and if that is the case it is wonderful to have found a life line to sanity. But there must be many for whom it fails. The average success rate detailed in overseas surveys is 5%. To me as a layperson this figure does not seem great. Not something to be shouted from the rooftops.

Surely we must realize that AA is not the only solution. That one size does not fit all.

In this day and age we now have many choices in life. If we don't like your doctor we have every right to change to another. If we don't for any reason feel happy with the surgeon who is going to operate on us we can elect to pursue another.

We must be able to offer these people addicted to alcohol other methods of help.

If you have no faith or understanding of a God based system, that everyone says can help you, and are skeptical from the outset, the struggle to achieve a positive result will always be an impossible task.

It is heartening to know that others have walked this road looking for alternative ways of helping the alcoholic, other than sending them to AA or a 12 step program.

In offering the following books to read, I wish to emphasize that there are alternatives that are effective.
No one way is the only way.

Different strokes for different folks.
The more choices that can be offered, I hope the more people can be helped.

Further reading and Websites

www.aanottheonlyway.com – Melanie Solomon

www.sossobriety.org

www.orange-papers.org

www.passagesmalibu.com

When AA Doesn't Work for You: Rational Steps to Quitting
Alcohol   - Albert Ellis

How to Stay Sober: Recovery without Religion
                                        - James Christopher

Many Roads, One Journey: Moving beyond the 12 Steps
                                          - Charlotte Davis Kasl

The Truth about Addiction and Recovery
                                    - Stanton Peele & Archie Brodsky

Sober for Good – New Solutions for Drinking Problems
                                          - Anne Fletcher

Addiction, Change and Choice: The New View of Alcoholism
                                      - Vince Fox

The Myth of Alcoholism as a Disease – Herbert Fingarette

Alcohol: How to Give Up and Be Glad You Did – Philip Tate

The Final Chapter

In September 2006 my husband had to retire from work. In December of the same year he sold his house and moved to a smaller coastal property where he hoped to pursue his love of fishing.

In February 2007 he had a major fall which resulted in hospitalization for a wound to the head. By April his digestion was very poor, with frequent nausea and vomiting. His legs had swollen enormously from the knees down and walking was very difficult.
He visited his doctor regularly looking for a quick medical fix, but not wanting, or being able to stop the alcohol, which was the root of the now extreme medical problems.

Although by September 2007 the swelling in his legs had reduced, the pain in the feet had increased. He described it as being constantly stung by bees when he walked. The feet would also alternate between intense burning sensations to freezing cold, but in both instances he became left with a near numbness when walking. He slept in short naps of no longer than an hour at a time, as he was continually woken with sharp stabbing pains in his legs. He could no longer bear bedclothes, footwear or clothing to touch his feet, so the mere action of moving his legs became excruciating.

He used to be a big man weighing 17 stone [108kg] but between February and September 2007 he lost 3 stone [21kg] and all muscle tone.
His short term memory had deteriorated and he had to rely on writing everything down in order to remember.
His heart also raced when doing the simplest of tasks and he was forced to rest often.

It was extremely distressing to watch this person who was deeply loved, slowly deteriorating with every drink.

In sober moments I discussed this quietly with him.

He couldn't see it. What was I going on about? Was I mad?

It was only in the last week of his life that he said "I think I have really stuffed up my body" and "the alcohol has really taken its toll."

He knew how ill he had become, but in his usual manner as regards to his health, chose to take the path of – if you completely ignore the problem it isn't really happening.

This man who was employed as a problem solver was the complete opposite when it came to his own life.

Kevin died peacefully in his sleep 28 October 2007.

At Rest

Think of me as one at rest
For me you should not weep
I have no pain, no troubled thoughts
For I am just asleep
The living, thinking me that was
Is now forever still
And life goes on without me
As time forever will

If your heart is heavy now
Because I've gone away
Dwell not long upon it friend
For none of us can stay
Those of you that liked me
I sincerely thank you all
And those of you that loved me
I thank you most of all

The answer to life's riddle
In life I never knew
I go with hope that now I will
And even so will you
Oh foolish, foolish me that was
I who was so small
To have wondered, even worried
At the mystery of it all

And in my fleeting life span
As time went rushing by
I found some time to hesitate
To laugh, to love, to cry
Matters it now if time began
If time will ever cease?
I was here, I used it all
And now I am at peace.

In closing all I can hope is that after reading this book there will be someone out there who will be helped.

In fairness to Kevin the text that follows is the address he gave, 18 months before his death, after completing an eight week residential program.

"Hi my name is Kevin and I am an alcoholic.

I've sat where you are for the last eight Tuesdays nights and while I have enjoyed each occasion I have also wondered what I would say on my graduation or even would I say anything.

However here I am which goes to prove that you can teach old dogs new tricks.

I can use that phrase as young James and I both had birthdays while on the program.

Respecting the confidentiality rule I can only say that I am now 58, but when we arrived I was three times older than him. I wonder how different my life would have been if I had sought help at his age.

Before I go into the tricks I have now learnt I would like to explain why I needed to be here.

I started my love, or what I wrongly thought was love, for alcohol when I was 17. It was six o'clock closing then but I and my workmates prided ourselves in being able to leave work at 5pm and down three jugs of beer each in the one hour allowed. The fact that it only cost what is now $1.00 didn't help.

From that time on I systematically moved on to wine and spirits. I even dabbled in home brew when finances were limited.

I met my future wife, who is here tonight, and we married when we were both young. Two years later we had a beautiful daughter who to my delight was my constant shadow for many years, along with alcohol of course.

Over the years I was lucky enough to have a loving wife who could not do more for me, a loving daughter, a handful of great friends, a nice home and a well paid job that I really enjoyed. The icing on the cake was two beautiful granddaughters.

However I was never too far away from alcohol throughout all of that. There weren't many days in my life that went by without me indulging. It all seemed to turn to custard around 2000. Even six months of chemotherapy and beating cancer only slowed me down for a while.

My life was a downward spiral.

Insanely I chose alcohol over everything else and the pace of my slide got faster and faster.

In the last eighteen months my wife of 33 years left me after finally accepting that she couldn't put up with my drinking and broken promises any more.

My daughter became too fearful to answer her phone in case it was her drunken Dad, my granddaughters often thought their Granddad was silly and smelt funny and all but two of my friends avoided me.

Twice I needed to be detoxed in Pitman House and once at Cornwall Park hospital. Early this year I ended up in Auckland hospital twice in quick succession. I am told I threatened ambulance staff, doctors and nurses.

I had to have a minder assigned to me because of my irrational behavior.

It finally sunk in that I had a real problem when a specialist told me that I was slowly but surely committing suicide with each drink.

But I am a slow learner and even after being accepted for this program I thought I'd better make the most of it while waiting to start and I managed to get into trouble for the first time.
That put my job, which I had been in since leaving school, into jeopardy.
I had reached the pits and the only way out for me was oblivion or the Salvation Army.
Luckily on the 27 March along I came to Ewington Avenue.

I'm now ever so thankful that I did. After eight weeks the light at the end of my tunnel is no longer a freight train coming head on towards me.

I sincerely thank the Salvation Army and every member of the staff for giving me this opportunity. Thanks also to my peers, both past and present for their support and companionship.

Special thanks to Warren, my counselors and all the other counselors who facilitate the group sessions.
Linda B our chats have been invaluable and while I can't clearly define my Higher Power yet, I believe you have put me on the right track.

To Cherry, my wife thanks for everything. I now understand and accept your decision.
To Linda, my boss thanks to you and to my employer for the support and encouragement given to me. Thanks also to Rob my work colleague and friend.

I can't let this opportunity go by without also mentioning my assignment to the duty of cleaning pots for three of the eight weeks that I have been here. Rightly or wrongly I put that down to an administrative error rather than my errant smoking habits. Thanks Robert.

And finally to some of the more important tricks this old dog has learnt.

Be honest, both internally and externally, set clear boundaries, say no when appropriate and think through any problems rather than ignore or rush into them.

In closing I wish each of you well in whatever journey you are taking and I hope you safely reach your chosen destination.

Thank you.

In 2008 I self published the first small print run of this book under the title 'My Concrete Umbrella' here in New Zealand, which sold well.

Sadly I received many emails from people who said they felt they were reading their own life story.

A lot of people wished they had read my book earlier.

Several brave folk sent me their personal stories. Some had harrowing stories and a few had great success.

We need to know we are not alone, and that others have plodded along the same path, and somehow reached a less stressful place.

We, the partners of these addicted drinkers, have to have a life. It may not be the life we imagined we were going to have. It will be a different life.

Index for

Please note:

The author is not a counselor, doctor, therapist, psychologist, psychiatrist, life coach or health professional. This book is my own personal opinion gleaned from living with an alcoholic partner, my husband.

It is not the intention of the author to provide any type of counseling in this book.
The opinions offered and thoughts conveyed, are those of the author.
No responsibility or liability can be accepted by the author for any actions taken by any person or organization.
If you fear for your own safety seek a safe refuge.
In an emergency the front of the phone book lists numbers for urgent help.

www.cherryparker.co.nz

Notes :

Made in United States
Orlando, FL
05 March 2023

30651138R10048